How to Start-Up

a Food Truck Business

By Hitachi Choparazzi

How to Start-Up a Food Truck Business

©Copyright 2020

All Rights Reserved

By Hitachi Choparazzi

Chop-A-Style Publishing LLC

LCCN: 2022902453

ISBN: 979-8-9857661-0-3

Acknowledgements

To all the people who have dreams to be independent and entrepreneurs that love to service people and express themselves in food freedom. Now you can own and maintain a successful mobile food service with a menu of your choice. I acknowledge you for taking the initiative to pursue your own path and taking actions to achieve your food dreams.

ATTN:

This How to *Start-Up a Food Truck* Business is only to be used as a guide to implement successful practices, safety, food management, and tips of dos and don'ts. This book is not meant as a guarantee that your actual food truck start-up will be an instant success. This how-to book is to simplify and show you merely guidance in a correct format and articulate chronological order for your best interest for successful start-up, fees, research, inspections, and sanitation hazards.

Contents

- Chapter 1 -

"Research"

You want to start-up a food truck, research is first. Research is you doing your homework of what is actually the real pieces, cost, time, and the know-how to get the business operational. You can create your food truck business plan, look up all the data points, right audience, and location hot spots.

Research is you really taking the proper time out to thoroughly do your homework of proper preparation. The actualization it gives you is a tool to help you weave out all of those ideal images in your head that you believe to be realistic. It may be possible, but not safe or meet standard requirements, inspections, or simply illegal violations. This is not meant to rain on your parade or stop your creativity. It's meant to help you better your creativity, enthusiasms, and energy to be counterproductive on the right legit path. This takes you one step closer to you achieving your vision of success, which also saves you time and money on costly wrong mistakes. Therefore, your due research is also used as a corrective action implementation. A preventive measure.

The next question is how do you know what to look up and if it's the right research? There is all-around general food truck start-ups info, then domesticated. You want to research the state, city, and county that's applicable to where you want to start-up first. Be careful not to get caught up online doing research subjects to lead you to frivolous rabbit holes. People will try to click-bait you and sell you bogus things that's not even relevant to your cause, brand, or state with food trucks.

You have to execute with a plan of action and making the right decision and seeing what works versus what don't work or people telling you. A business plan is not required to start-up your own food truck. However, it's highly recommended because the business plan helps you to organize, prioritize, and structure a food truck operational blueprint and foodprint. Like your hiring, staffing, cost of operations including inventory and all overhead. Overhead like truck maintenance and other expenses that may occur that you did not plan or see there prior to start-up, that people don't tell you that's usually learnt thru hands-on experience. Most people during all major start-ups have these type of expenses, challenges, occurrences which most don't tell you. Instead they let you make the same costly and time-consuming mistakes. After all, they are your competitors, threaten you could take them out of business or their customers, too.

Therefore, your business plan acts as your map of accountability and operations. Search them thoroughly. Search your crowd for the people and what type of food or dish you catering to. See if there are similar food trucks in your same state or area. See what they doing and do it better, make your dish better, possibly even lower the cost or add more to the dish portions. Maybe even add a dessert to top them off. You have to have a different point of uniqueness to complement your services to people. Giving them ultimate experiences with food critique and hosting. Your outside lobbying and waiting time of delivery to hand and your food truck appealing image is everything that all evolves from due research. Remember research is the basis of you getting factual information to have factual real-time results.

You would search all your main food dishes, domestic or exotic, that you want to serve on your menu for customer selection and preference. Look up the time it takes to cook each dish and the cost of each dish to make. Look up the average prices for your other food truck competitors with that same dish or menu. Make sure whatever you decide to cook goes with your truck premise and brand. For example, if you have a chicken-n-waffle food truck, you don't want to be popular with a line around the corner for your pizza. You want it to match your dish, brand, and message for people to spread the word of mouth with excellent one-of-a-kind 5-star reviews or for having a chicken-n-waffles special cupcake with your chicken-n-waffle food truck being the only one in your zoning area with an exclusive add-on serving.

Therefore, it has to make sense and match going hand-to-hand. Research your outside entertainment like flatscreen TVs, a sound system, benches, stands, and seating. Mist systems if it's the summertime or you in those hot California, Arizona, Nevada, and Florida states. Anything you could possibly think of you want to do or innovate your food truck and leaving a signature style imprinting your food truck brand.

Now your food truck should have a theme, a sound, brand mantra, logo, or mascot. Like KFC has the Colonel, McDonald's has that "I'm loving it" mantra, Mountain Dew has feature rap artist background music and stating "Do the Dew." You must create your own company slogans, jingles, brand imagery, and taste that coordinates with your theme and sound. Of course these more franchise companies have millions of dollars into creatives and ad agencies to help them with brand image and staying relevant. However, you can do this just as well as any brand-name, big-house company, too. You have to do your research, brainstorm ideas, imagery, and food themes that will lead to the ultimate lasting or first impressions experience from your customers. Remember your consumers is what actually grows your food truck business and help spread the word organically without advertisement and promo budgets and out-of-pocket cost. This same ad money or radio advertisement money can go towards reinvestment back into the truck maintenance or inventory and paying employees.

An example of your food truck theme is, let's say you have done your thorough research on Caribbean food and built your Caribbean menu catering toward all West Indies or Caribbean Sea dishes exclusively. Then you would have a Caribbean theme like a Caribbean feel such as Caribbean music and videos playing outside, or your food truck wrapped in island scenery like coconut trees, white sandy beaches, etc. You can have your employees dressed in the laid-back islanders easy apparel, like those striped dreadlock hats, playing Bob Marley, giving them a taste of Caribbean experience in the inner city on lunch break from their stressful office or day job. It's about delivery. Once you understand, have the knowledge and willpower to research things that match your theme, truck, message, and menu, you are ready to take it to the next step to advance your research where you are really crossing your T's and dotting all of your I's, every single one, no ifs, maybes, or buts about it.

Advancing your research is you taking extra steps to foolproof your food truck operational business plan beyond basic research, like getting all the exact details and the loose ends, too. Some searches are open-ended, meaning they can go either way or different ways than your standard basic searches. You cannot have an inner narrative of saying, "Okay, that's enough. I got it at first take." Instead, tell yourself,

"I have got to search more beyond the surface because there has to be more to it."

For example, if you research zoning, fines, and fees, it may simply tell you all fees to register a trade name and logo of a food truck, fines from parking in front of a restaurant and violating time of parking your truck, maybe even the zoning radius of the approximately how many feet away from zoning restricted areas, businesses, and restaurants. You must also remember that restaurants are not fans of food trucks either and your competitor, especially with all these new up-and-coming food delivery services and apps. They are threatened by your truck, too. Check in your city, state, and county all the fees, fines, violating policy and dos and the don'ts critically. This is nothing to tread lightly with or doing light surface research, because most food truck violations like parking, zoning, timing, and restriction fines range from $1,500. That's more than majority of food trucks gross per day. Fines of violation will have your food truck business in the red or possibly shut down for operational use. I also see this in initial food truck starters. Shut down for health inspection, simple violations or hazardous violations like not having ventilation and hood system or having no sink in your food truck.

Some food trucks have fryers because it caters to their fried deep dishes of fish, fries, and chicken. I even see more people use air fryers for healthy choice of their customers versus all that fried grease and cooking oils. Your truck may not even require a fryer according to your menu food service, like if you doing a Southern Louisiana Cajun-style stewed gumbo. If you selling cups of multiple meat gumbos, then you do not need a fryer, but you should research the right cooking pots, stoves. Look up if you want to do propane, electric solar panels to generate your power, or a backup generator. You need to really be clear on your vision and what it takes to complete it. Education is key, especially in any field you're jumping head-first into. Most people don't have time to take a class, read a book, do all the intense research it takes, so they just Google how to start-up, then watch a quick food truck summary video, thinking they have got it and all the tools for having a successful, likeable, and lucrative number-one niche food truck in their town.

For every idea, there is a counterweight of fear, negativity and self-doubt saying it's impossible, especially without no resources, revenue, or prior experience in that particular space. Next you have people who take their ideas into action. However, they soon fail and business fails because they did not have the time to do research to improvise a proper effect plan or budget and overhead realistically. Then you have the successful ones who had an idea, researched, to action, executed with their business plan, built a fabulous team and scalable food trucks to franchise and other trucks in multiple locations and cities. Success matters.

Lastly is the budget. You need to have actualization dealing with your budget cost of operations and all underlying expenses. You cannot keep running to friends and family for a loan, being short on unexpected cash due to food shortage and unexpected repairs that you did not occur in your overhead percentage, mainly from following online content and quick videos. Again, you have to put your thorough research and time in to discover the ins and outs of the food truck business they do not tell you or disclose in fine print. You want to do your research to help enable to make your food truck imprint like your own signature thumbprint. You want to be known for good service, good food, good experience, great customer service. The best.

- Chapter 2 -

"Discovery & Innovation"

Next stages are discovery and innovation. They are both key start-up elements applicable to any start-up business. First, you have to discover what you want to pursue and how you want to pursue it. Then learn how to innovate and integrate it to work for you versus against you in a systematic way until it's automatic. In this chapter I will show you how to do discovery, framework, and innovational cues and skillsets to formulate right fits adaptive to you.

Discovery is about your gift, passion, and superpower all align to create a vision to bring forth. Some people are inspired, motivated, but non-reactive because they simply do not know how to tap in and bring out their unique cause, talent, gift. Some people have gifts of seeing what others don't see, like an idea or between the gaps of an untapped market. For instance, you can deliver a whole new element that most food truck vendors or customers have yet to be seen and actually concoction brilliantly. However, the problem lies in how do you bring that out, especially if it's complex or diverse. How to connect and convert to build on that idea and form a vision to act on is thru discovery.

The first key element into fine discovery is journaling, notes, and writing things and ideas down. Logging it in your phone is even better than storing it in your head. Remember, the dullest pencil is better than the sharpest mind. Also, if you can think it, you must ink it. We get over 50k thought processes a day, not including how your subconscious mind goes on repeat and rewind autopilot when you are asleep. Therefore, even if you have to leave a pen and pad next to your bed to jot down even out of a snoring sleep, it's worth it and a great practice of good habit. Some of the greatest creators, innovators, scientists all had notes they would write down during the day and night out of sleep. Discovery makes your creative brain waves electrify. It's up to you to catch them.

Next in discovery is focus. Whatever you focus on, you will get thru the law of attraction. Like if you tell yourself, "Look for blue trucks," your mind will pay attention to every blue truck possible on the road, parked, at events, etc. It's the same way what you seek, you shall find. Your mind works better than Google. You just have to search with key discovery topics, words, and subjects you desire. Your mind retrieves information at lightning speed, too. Say, for instance, if I say the word "Saturn," you'll automatically see the picture of the Saturn rings to formulate in your thinking process. Therefore, all your thought processes are most retrieved information from your brain. You learn how to focus more in discovery by tuning out the noise and mental clutter or world distractions. The mind goes from a beta wave to an alpha brain wave. A lot of people meditate to help reset their mind to refocus from their subconscious state to consciousness.

Then there is the developmental stage of discovery once you learnt or figured out how to grasp and hone the craft of discovery awareness. Your thoughts become your actions, and your actions manifest your thoughts. Believe in yourself and development of your discovery. Your development should first be to move yourself forward into action. Then, you'll start to create your vision around your discovery. Next you dominate your development space to a skilled action. Your development will help drive you into creating your space into actual reality. That same insight light or inner passion, desire, and fire comes from that tingle sensation of discovery dying to manifest and thrive.

You write down or use your mobile device to put all your pros and cons about your new discovery and desire to build on it. You will weave out the impossible versus probable. Sometimes when you read things back or say things out loud to yourself, you have a different outlook or standing point. You may decide against it or for it. Maybe to integrate it or innovate on the logic.

A story and example of discovery is, after the late great Kobe Bryant and his daughter passed, this guy and his daughter wanted to pay homage and do some type of tribute. Then he had discovered a way to honor Kobe with a Kobe Bryant Tribute food truck. He painted his food truck purple with yellow Lakers theme, a mural of Kobe and daughter GiGi, along with the jersey numbers eight, twenty-four, and two for GiGi. A percentage of the proceeds goes to a girls' basketball foundation, which I think is helluva brilliant because he discovered a way to do a tribute, feed people, and give back to charity a contribution. The public backed him up with a long line just to get a Black Mamba hot dog and a Mambacita Chili Jalapeño fries. All while giving you a Staples Center experience. Genius with a need, cause, effect, and plan of action executed perfectly and successfully with an outpouring of support.

That is how you build on your discovery from that initial thought process to action. The key element is to evolve that thought process. It may take 2 hours, 2 days, or 2 years. It just depends on you. It's no specific time or pressure on you to evolve it. Long as you write down or log each of your steps and path to success and dreams into sure reality. You don't have to tell nobody your ideas, dreams, vision, or plans of actions. They can hate, prolong you, or have negative feedback, which all leads to self-doubt, and self-doubt is the same as self-sabotaging. However, on the flip side of that, some common belief practices believe in speaking things into action with the power you give to your words and thought process to being. Also it's for accountability, too. When you state something to others, friends, or online, they will all hold you to that and accountable for every word, goal, and visions you claimed. Stay facts and stick to them.

Now that you have an idea and structure upon manifesting your discovery, we will move on into innovation. The correct definition of innovation is to introduce something new, a new idea, method, or device to primarily make changes to. It's like, can you make something good better? Can you redesign a design to greater heights and greatness? To be an innovator, you have to be open-minded to do, act, and see what others don't, then be able to formulate that to your speed, style, or preference to introduce to the world. This is the same way how emails, smartphones, lightbulbs, and so much more modern world breakthroughs happen. The discovery is what helps you transform your innovation into a breakthrough.

First you have to see a problem to be solved and fix it or make it better, maybe even introduce something entirely new to the world. It can even be a practical process that you find a way to innovate and make better by being easier and more convenient to people, especially nowadays in this instant-gratification era we live in with everybody being too spoiled and wanting the easiest and simple way possible.

Now the question you ask yourself is, How can I make my food truck different or better and introduce something new to the market? What type of food can I innovate? What theme can I innovate? What new system of cooking or food method can I concoction and innovate? How can I innovate my menu or venue? How can I innovate my truck appearance to have my exterior very impressive with added and different features than the food truck parked right next to me or within my zoning areas?

Then you simply answer those same questions with a solution form by a reverse engineering technique, where you tackle the problem in reverse. For example, if you take something apart by disassembling it, you'll see all the parts and components that make it work. What if, by looking at it thru a reverse standpoint, you actually spot a problem and have a quick hack or solution to make it work better, faster, and more efficiently? It's just like that Kobe Bryant food truck. He innovated and integrated a Kobe tribute, Lakers theme, Black Mamba hot dog, and GiGi Chili Mambacita fries along with giving you the ultimate Staples Center experience with Lakers music playing and games showing of Kobe, too. That has innovation written all over it while giving back to girls' basketball foundation, a good deed all in one. There are plenty of food trucks, but only one Kobe Bryant Tribute food truck and dish.

Therefore innovation is not just in you, it is you and your ideas, visions, and endless possibility of your dreams you had for years. You can also train yourself and trigger your brain to innovate, like framework of thinking and how you think. Do you think with an equation? Or do you see what others can't, or won't? You first need to train yourself to look for the gaps, spot them, and fill in the blank. Just like reading emojis and able to read between the lines. It takes practice, but you have to be aware of it first. Then, in order to be aware, you have to again be conscious of it. For example, you may say 2 plus 2 equals 4, and I may say no. Also 6 minus 2 equals 4, 3 plus 1 equals 4, 12 minus 8 equals 4, and so on. That's seeing different from most and training yourself to think all around. The natural gifted innovators are natural problem solvers or passionate people. They have passion projects or obsessed with solving a particular problem. Innovators fail time and time again, but they still put in the effort they see in their head until they innovate it right or correctively. They are relentless and strive relentlessly, and that's the same attitude and push you, too, need to have to truly innovate successfully.

Write down your passions, your dreams, and how you want to apply them into your personal food truck and incorporate your style or new method or system. Like if you only wanted to do a drink service smoothie food truck, maybe you can integrate a few pastries to the menu, or bagels. Or you can have a food truck that offers both a drink and food service. Innovate any style you wish long as it works. Also, you can use a method of looking for a demand, like a certain type of food, taste, or drink that's rare, imported, or exotic that's hard to get exclusive rights to and limited. That's looking for those gaps like we have discussed previous. You could look for native foods for different continents. An Amazon or Brazil cuisine people have not tested in the United States yet, or maybe even a rare African fruit that people have to go deep to pick and find the ripe ones. This is all samples of pure innovation and thinking as a true innovator does.

However, I cannot tell you what's right for you or your dreams, visions, and passions. That is totally up to you. I can only give you a blueprint of how to be innovative to your best ability to follow it. Develop your uniqueness of discovery and innovation with your signature brand and food truck that people cannot compete hard with.

- Chapter 3 -

"Niche Food Dish"

The heart of every food truck is the niche food dish. This whole truck food base of operational service all cater around the one specific food premise dish. Now that you've done all your research and understand how to work on discovery and innovate, you can work on creating your unique food dish.

This niche food dish is the first part of building your food truck business before actually spending revenue and buying a food truck, equipment, and inventory. You have to be clear on what you want to cook and what taste you aiming for your crowd. If you aiming for sweet and savory taste or any other unique concoction, they all have to be tasted, sampled, and tested. Start with friends, family, and co-workers first to sample your dishes and test what works and what don't, what the like and what makes them frown. A likable food dish will make their tastebuds tingle and dance, which signals the brain to release the dopamine chemical of the reward system and cravings. That creates them wanting more and craving your dish for different days to come later on.

However, this response and reaction from friends and family needs to be modest and non-biased. They cannot tell you it's fine and tastes just right. Instead, you need people to tell you the honest truth and "no" if it's not up to par or too bland and awful or nasty taste concoction. The solution is for you to go beyond friends and family for feedback and start reaching out to your community and neighborhood events to give you honest feedback. Your neighbors are some of the best and worst food critics. Please do share with them and make you a spreadsheet to keep track of all people that liked or did not like each dish by gender and age group or geography. You can even keep track of ethnic backgrounds, too, that resonate with more cultural food dishes. However, in order to really measure it successfully, that system needs to be at least a hundred people to evaluate and rate your dish to the best possibilities and positive results. Remember, this is the first real test you conquer and then start-up and build your food truck from the inside out. Stimulate your appetite with a delicious pleasing taste of satisfaction is essential to begin.

Next we will get into how to find your unique, creative, special niche food dish. This again is your food truck lifeline. You can use a family or traditional rare recipe that already has generational approval passed down thru decades on end. Or you can go online and research some valid recipes of your choice or liking. You can find certain chefs or culinary experts to help you cook, prepare, or certify recipes you want to create and concoction, as long as it all works and people can validate it as a great taste for success. If you even want to do appetizers, you can look up a pastry chef to assist you, too. They all usually inexpensive unless they are celebrity chefs and hosts.

Maybe you want to do a vegan food truck and want to create a vegan chili dish or a plant-based dish, and you don't know where to start at. Most people have the lack of understanding on plant-based diets. However, now it's been the new wave trend, so it's definitely a space for it and a plant-based food truck. The task is to come up with a unique niche plant-based food dish, then evolve your menu around it with similar plant-based power dishes and plant-based add-on drinks, too. To all your new people trying out your plant-based diet for the first time testing out what all the hype is about, you need to leave a helluva first-time impression to give them a grade-A experience with your niche plant-based dish. Also, you can have a chart outside your food truck of plant-based diet fun facts for all newcomers or people that just began plant-based, like organic, stress on the planet, animal torture and slaughterhouses, massive productions, cost, taste, and accessibility, too. Those are the main fears and reasons behind people going plant-based diets that most non-plant-based people don't know or educate and research. Therefore, it's totally up to you how you cater, service, and your niche dish captivates.

You want your dish to be a crowd-pleaser and craving. Your special niche dish should have people standing and waiting in long lines gladly. You don't want to be like that food truck parked at the rodeo or state fair. That line is always empty with only one person cooking, serving, and working the register that everyone walks right past gladly. You want your food truck to thrive based solely on your niche food dish. A good dish will sell itself, no doubt about that, without no exclusive marketing. Maybe indirect marketing like how people start spreading word of the mouth telling a friend and they tell a friend, too. People will be adding you to their InstaStories and SnapChats. Also you'll be getting tons of high 5- and 4-star reviews online, too.

A prime example of a good food product doing indirect marketing was Popeyes first chicken sandwich. It had drove people into a frenzy. It had people standing in lines sleeping outside, fist fights, and going crazy just for the anticipation of a taste. Most people haven't even had a true taste or feel of the chicken sandwich yet. The demand was high and had the United States in a new chicken sandwich phenomenon that couldn't supply with the demand, and they ran out of buns and chicken. After a few months it came back to the market and a permanent spot on Popeyes menu. The people went on another frenzy for the first 30 days until it died down. Then Popeyes did a target marketing commercial with real people recording their viral reactions to finally getting a sandwich to taste. This was to keep it fresh on those other people's mind that haven't had a chance to experience the new chicken sandwich because of all the long lines, heavy traffic, and drama behind the crazy and chaos created. Imagine if you can create a signature-style dish like that thru your niche.

Now, let's go back to the Kobe Bryant Tribute food truck. Let's focus on his niche dish of the Black Mamba hot dog. He knew he had to do a tribute hot dog in honor of Kobe's legacy that fits in with the Mamba mentality. So, he first went with an exceptionally large jumbo-size hot dog. He matched a taste of a similar hot dog to the ones served at the Staples Center. Then cut all his onions, peppers, and toppings in swirls in a slithering snake style. Then he went with black olives as the last toppings to give it an all-black exterior effect. He also complemented the Mamba hot dog with a black tray to hold the Mamba hot dog in, too. Even with his daughter GiGi's tribute Mexican-style chili jalapeño fries, giving it a Mambacita taste and experience with the similar framework with great result of a complementary gift dish on the menu with the Mamba hot dog, too.

Take a reverse look into how he managed to pull the whole Kobe Bryant tribute and ultimate experience work successful. If you think it was because of the pretty decked-out food truck or capitalizing off of a tragedy, you wrong. Remember he donates a percentage of his proceeds and profit margins to a girls' basketball foundation. Also if you guessed any other following reasons behind his success, you wrong, dealing with marketing or whatever else may come to your mind. The real success behind his Kobe Bryant tribute food is his great-tasting Mamba hot dog. He put all his devoted time, research, food analyst into crafting the best hot dog with a mixture of Chicago, New York, and California-Style hot dogs with multiple toppings and add-on how you like it. People love customization and having it their way, too. Imagine if he had some two-for-99-cent packet of frozen-aisle franks. How will bland keep your truck running or people coming back time and time again? The name of the food truck game is reoccurance customers and building a trust and relationship with your quality and delivery of your niche food dish to the public and your community. Then you will establish and build dedicated lifetime customer that will follow you and pull-up to support and promote your events. You maybe can even get some sponsors and influencers support, too, all just from your niche food dish. It's all possible, again with the right niche dish. Be better than your competitors and great at what you do to the max.

Okay, if you still confused asking yourself, "How do I know what is the right niche dish to start at?" You must first remember to do a valid taste test beyond family and friends to get honest rational feedback. Next tackle whatever food dish your gut tells you or that you desire, and see no similar dishes. Like if you want to bring an Ireland dish, Saudi Arabia, and Sri Lanka concoction, you need to have the courage to try it. Step out of the box, and don't be afraid to commit and test boundaries. Even if you want to try a Japanese sushi dish mixed with a Spanish element, just simply do it. You never know what hits big and very lucrative. People will definitely let you know if it's yuck or suck.

That's the reason you have your taste-tester for, to hold you accountable and to actualization of data facts.

You can even do online polls on your social media feeds to engage with people to vote Yes or No on the niche dishes you want to create prior. Or maybe even which one of the concoctions they like and would love to see come to fruition, voting on which they prefer to buy. It is so many ways to get people to engage for free and help out. Getting the crowd involved online is free, and you do not need money to waste on cooking and hiring chefs to concoct prototype sample dishes for the public to test if they not feeling it in the first place. All your bad niche dish ideas will help save using your valuable and precious resources by simply outsourcing correctly and effectively with the public crowd online support. Again this is nothing you rush. You cannot make something work that does not fit or match accordingly because taste buds don't lie. Some may be less or more sensitive, but they all will cue your brain for a good or bad yuck face response or bright sensational smile from mouth-gasms.

Finally, after you found your perfect niche creative dish, have it tested successfully, you need to make sure the title of your dish is suitable and goes with your food truck logo, brand, and theme message. It should all go hand-in-hand and complement each other. Just like the Kobe tribute food truck and dish did and all complied, too. Then you build your whole menu, truck, interior, and exterior around your title. Name your dish spot-on correctively.

There is a such thing as key words, buzzwords, and key titles. I am not saying it has to be immaculate or extraordinary. It just has to fit and match your dish to build upon everything else with your truck, brand, and theme all in the proper sequence that's not too complex that your guest customers can get the concept and taste along with an awesome experience from your titled food dish.

- Chapter 4 -

"Registration, Zoning, & Inspections"

Now that you have your operational food truck business plan, done your thorough research, and created your niche food dish, it's time to learn how to register your food truck, brand, and zoning, along with the inspections.

Once you have your food truck business name and logo, you register them with a trade name and trademark form in your local city and county. You can find these forms online or look at your State Department of Revenue, or Secretary of State, or state local business registration buildings. There is also Federal trademark and forms online that you can do at that level as well. IRS.gov you can get an E.I.N. (Employer Identification Number) for free. Some states require you to do a classified ad or publication of using the trade name for 30 days before you can open up a business account. Most setting up business accounts require your state trade name registration form or certificate copy proof and a minimum deposit from $100 to $500 to open up. They will give you a business account and usually a debit card or business credit card depending on the bank, credit union, or online banking qualifications. Every institution system is different. You have to search around first to see what fits your preference.

Next is you have to get your business license, too, if you want to sell additional things like shirts, pens, buttons, cups, etc., with your food truck logo merch, because it's all taxes, too. Other states require you register a vendors license for your food truck as well. You will get a transaction tax privilege license. Then you can do payroll and keep track of daily, weekly, and quarterly earnings to document on your quarterly wages earning documents to record for the state taxes.

Most trucks don't have incorporations or S-corps. Some of the food trucks do have LLC, which is limited liability company, which looks professional and makes better so nobody cannot attack your food truck with lawsuits that will sue you as an individual. That will be devastating because they can take all your personal assets, bank account revenue including savings. This is why the LLC protects you from your livelihood, personal property, and belongings. However, you can register your food truck business under a sole proprietorship if you choose to. Proprietorship just means an owner. Remember, as a sole proprietorship, you are more reliable and responsible as an individual. However, you do not have to register an incorporation or LLC to start a food truck, you can simply check that sole proprietorship box. An incorporation is for a bigger scalable company, usually with a lot of employees, benefits, that you plan to be acquired by a bigger company or eventually do a public IPO stock market approach. Inc is usually for organizations, not food trucks, but you can scale and register for your Inc., if you so desire.

Next in food trucks there is a such thing is called zoning, and you have to have zoning permits in most states for food trucks. They may give you an area of sections you are only allowed to serve in, or it can also include timing in zoning, too. It may be a zoning chart with red areas you are allowed to park your truck. Whereas, other states may require you to take a zoning course before you get your zoning required permits for clearance. You should look all this info on zoning up online with your state and exclusive county guidelines and prerequisite for zoning. A prerequisite is something required beforehand or also for the end in view, too.

Zoning is to arrange in or mark off into different zones, especially to divide as a city into sections reserved for different purposes. There also are certain zoning violations that you need to know and should inquire about, too. These violations usually have hefty fines. You'll soon find out that the food industry is not food truck friendly and imposes a lot of fines and fees along with obstacles dealing with food truck start-ups and food trucks license, registrations, inspections. You must remember, food trucks is a new popular fast-growing side hustle that big companies and investors are threatened heavily by inferior of them not filling their restaurants and fast food franchise chains. Therefore, being aware of all zoning restrictions and how they all work is very important because it will save you violation sanctions and ridiculous fines like the previous example of parking your food truck within a few yards radius of a restaurant, food store, or even a place of business is all zoning violations, being parked outside your zones or not having your zoning permit for being in a certain district zone that your food truck is not registered or permitted to park and serve in.

It's also a such fine for solicitation, too, for soliciting other entity's consumers, like if you parked in front of an event or stadium without permission to entice or influence their audience or customers without due permission is a big fine and violating of zoning. Instead you need to have people doing these events, parties, markets, or venues request you to host your food truck service. Leave them an email or private social media message telling them if you meet the zoning requirements, you can host and accept their timeframes and dates for your truck to host their events, or you can simply use this same method for you in reverse, meaning you can look at your zoning areas and then send your food truck résumé and reviews for service, customer service, food quality and being able to cater to large crowds timely and effectively, too. Once they respond to your email or private social media message on one of those platforms, they will tell you yes or no. If yes, then it all worked out for the best and opened up a door of opportunity to build on a future service of catering businesship to host more events for them. Building a household relationship where you will generate more referrals and leads to host the most. If they decline your email offer to host your food truck at their events, still thank them with a reply email for their time and move on to the next request while keeping it professional. Remember, keep your food truck as professional and serious as possible. Treat it like a 5-star business, even though it's a mobile small food service.

Next we will get into inspections. Inspections are very important for being able to get your food truck legit, safe, and up and running, you have to pass all inspections. There is an operational inspection that's required to run your food truck, including safety. Then there is the Department of Health inspections dealing with food and health, making sure you don't get nobody sick, spreading disease or bacteria. You can, again, look up in your state and county the County Department of Health requirement beforehand. This way you would know what to expect and prepare for or simply what not to do. You can be implementing the wrong thing, system, or exposing your food and people to health hazards. Please do your thorough investigation and have a walk-thru by a professional or food consultant to see if they see any extra food violations you doing wrong that is an inspection violation before your food inspections. You can get a failed inspection fast and deemed unoperational to open up and serve people. The County Board of Health usually has sanctions for failed inspection like time restrictions before you can apply for your food truck operational license. The inspections is the main element of your food truck operation and licenses. Basically, the heart of all prerequisite for food trucks start-ups.

The overview is mandatory. First you see what the Health Department in your county requirements are to get inspected and code. The health board inspections and zoning permits. The inspection is to view closely and critically to examine your food truck and stations to make sure they meet regulatory standards.

The next thing you need to know and have for all your standard food trucks to fit inspection compliance are heating, ventilation, and hood systems, including a dual sink to wash your hands, too. Ventilation and a hood system for smoke to go out of by law is mandatory requirements, especially if your food truck uses a fryer or cooking, period. You also can hire local plumbers doing side jobs to install your sink system correctly and inexpensive with a direct waterflow course and drainage. A stainless sink is highly recommended. You can find all equipment online like eBay or Craigslist used or new, which we will address in the chapters to come, of all what is needed for your particular truck and where to look for them new versus used.

It is the same for all your wiring, hiring an electrician to run your truck power source direct and accordingly to pass inspections. Whether you choose to use an 11k power diesel generator to power the whole truck independent, or using solar panels conversion direct energy power of outsourcing. Maybe even hooking up your propane system directly and efficiently so that you don't set your whole truck on fire up in flames before you can be successful and see the return on your investment or flip another truck, too. Lastly, you don't want to blow yourself or anybody else up from propane leaks or not knowing how to regulate or a possible employee disperse the propane accordingly, too. Again, you want to do all your thorough research on all of these options, requirements, and inspections prerequisite. You need to be up to par by all means necessary for true success in your food truck start-up.

Lastly of this chapter, we will get into insurance. Getting your truck insured is a must. You may not be able to get your food truck bonded. However, you can get the best insurance coverage possible. You can get a combined business insurance and with your regular car insurance. Or you can simply get a regular food truck insurance premium policy. It's optional and totally up to you. Having a food truck with no insurance or expired insurance is a huge fine, which will result in your truck being parked and illegal to drive around town. You don't want to put all this research, time, sweat equity, and money into a food truck start-up and it flops because of fines, lack of proper insurance. You would think it sounds like a no-brainer. However, some people really think they do not need an insurance policy on their food truck because it will be parked most of the time because they are not serving dishes in mid-day traffic. Even if it's liability, you still need truck insurance. A lot of people make this mistake, especially think it's too expensive. Remember even if your truck gets into a fender bender, you're solely liable.

Now key notes and takeaways of this final process for this fourth chapter of registrations, zoning, and inspections by code. First, you want to start out by calling the local Health Department or online site and what the requirements are and build your truck around it. Have your truck built per the code to pass inspections. Next, your food service handle certification and food management certification are the two permits needed and required by law to operate your food truck. It's usually taking classes to get certified with a manager certification. The start-up food truck fees should include all manager food safety courses, the LLC and tax ID, including inspection fees. An LLC is not required, it's just risk management.

- Chapter 5 -

"Menus & Venues"

Building your menu is essential to your food truck. A menu should be clear and easy to read, including the prices per dish or entrees. Some trucks have their menu selections in decals outside of their truck exterior, very bright and big for customers waiting in line can see and use for selection of choice or to try a new dish menu feature. It can be new or a temporary limited taster. Other trucks have their menu selection from inside of the truck on a board drawing or chart hanging up. Some even use TVs to display their menu outside of their trucks, too.

The food truck's menu is what their successful revenue comes from. How well you set-up your menu is key, too. Some people put their best top dishes first and the more expensive dishes last. Whereas, other truck owners do the exact opposite by putting their most expensive dishes first and their lavish ones last. A data analytical recent study shows people usually select the first few top 3 things they see off the menu. These are called behavior pattern traits. Now you be the judge to how you want to do your specific menu set-up order by the data. Use it effectively, think about your menu set-up order how it will cater to your customers, fit, and work strategically.

You can even use fancy lettering or words that goes with your food truck theme and logo, too. Like, for example, if you have a hot dog food truck, you should name your menu offerings after them, like the onion dog, relish dog, or the sauerkraut dog. It's about menu etiquette and loving to serve people. The more appealing, the more satisfaction of the customers. Your menu should not be messy or too cluttered and hard to read. It should be precise and list all of the services and prices you offer, including specials, too. Maybe your words are too small and a senior citizen cannot read them off the menu and you lose a customer and get a bad review, which reviews spread like wildfire and are very effective and contagious. They can be used for you or against your food truck ratings and reputation. Remember your reputation is everything and highly reputed in any household brand and business. However, a good review and reputation is based on your service, taste, and the customer experience you give them.

A menu is a valid up-to-date list of all dishes available to order or a list of offerings and options like meals, drinks, and advertisers. How you stack it and present your menu is totally up to you and whatever style or format works in your food truck interest.

Next, let's show you how to build upon your food truck menu. First you want to write out on paper a list of pros and cons or dos and don'ts. What will work and not work or goes against your brand, theme, or niche dish. Do not make your list on menu practice complex or extensive. If you place 21 separate items you offer as entrées, you may not be able to keep up with the demand timely. This is where you end up spending more cooking time than actualization of the serving time, which is a train wreck and recipe for failure of start-up within the first opening week. Obviously that's something you mark off your list of what not to do on your menu. On the other hand, if you have

21 things listed on your menu that's not solely cooking dishes, like drinks, desserts, ready-made and pre-cooked items is doable, if you can really manage a fast serve time turnover rate. If you can handle the customer service aspect, then of course mark your 21 items listed on the paper a go-ahead. However, you have to test it out first to see if it works or you can develop an effective customer service system with employees to make it work. If not, you must be able to make little menu adjustments or modify.

Now you want to build on your main niche dish and dishes similar around that. You want to put your money-makers and the quickest dishes to make as top rank priority on your menu exclusively. Then, work on your way down that list of what's more important dish that meets your food truck brand standard needs and won't have the crowd of consumers lost in the sauce. There also is a such thing as mix-matching of crossbranding gone wrong. This is where you try to incorporate a certain style to concoction with your food truck dish, but it does not work nor fit. It's called bad integration acceptance, where the consumer objects to the peculiar odd menu item, dishes, or options. You can tell because this is the least sought, sold, or favorite item. These are menu eyesores that you should hurry up and kindly remove and abolish from your menu before it cramps it and cripples your business. Remember your menu selections have to be named after what your food truck can be identified with or related to. No need to over-think and make too complex. It can be sophisticated though exclusively.

Let's use a few different Las Vegas food truck menus for example. One was a mobile coffee food truck that catered to the Vegas international conventions and international tourist crowd. It had a multiple international coffee selection from different countries and continents ranging from lattes, mochas, frappuccinos, all in that country's style and flavor of brewed coffee and traditions to give people that demographic experience of Nicaraguan, Peruvian coffee of all blends. Their menu fit just right and they had a lot on it, but could match and meet all their demands.

Next example was the Area 51 food truck. It had a green alien logo and spaceship flying saucer theme. Now every single item they offered on their short menu was some sort of extraterrestrial food name very creative. Like Saturn fries, and Orion onion rings, or the Martian milkshake, which all their unique named menu items listed made people want to try them out just to say they have or give them the ultimate Area 51 experience of alien and extraterrestrial based. This was one of the best themes and food truck marketing genius targeted to a specific crowd targeted audience that love to indulge in extraterrestrial phenomena and experience. To this day, they have a huge profit margin and food truck success.

Now that you understand how to successfully build your menu options with selective price features and your fancy add-ons we will move into the flyers. Flyers can be in any colors and printed online or Kinko's and Staples or any printing shop. Each flyer should consist of your food truck name, theme, logo, and menu list and prices. You can pass them out with each dish you serve or pay people to pass them out around town like malls, neighborhoods, or a targeted business place. I would recommend that you do bright colorful flyers to stand out. Make sure your social media handles on all platforms are listed of your food truck to follow and a contact info like a business line. Flyers are the same equivalent of a business card, even though you can have business cards, too. The flyers are bigger and can hold more than a business card. Also, it's harder to lose. Even if your flyer gets taken off the windshield and thrown away, it still gets looked at or read into someone's head, which is a prime example of brand awareness. It's all worth it, and we will get into more of the brand awareness and marketing side in the chapters to come.

Let's jump into the venues. A venue is a place where any events are usually held, ranging from music, festivals, markets, wedding receptions, etc. Venues are primary to food trucks along with business plazas, warehouse, and construction sites, too. This could be an annual or daily and maybe even a weekend gig that you pull your food truck up to host and cater to people. For instance, the Southwestern Mexican-style food truck pulls up from 11 a.m. to 1 p.m. for lunchtime hours at the industrial warehouse area. He caters to a certain venue at a certain time. These venues are essential for your food truck revenue. Some are worth it, others are not worth your time because you may barely break even. A lot of food trucks cost at least $500 to $1.5k a day to pull out, ranging from food, operational, and truck cost. Therefore, if you not going to at least double that to start-up your truck and rollout to a venue.

The key is to secure a venue or multiple venues to create constant revenue. The secret is to know how to secure a venue successfully. First you want to go out where everybody goes to. Establish a relationship and good reputation of taste and service. It's not just simple as passing out flyers, expecting to get lucky and the phone rings off the hook for bookings. You must initiate contact with venues' organizers, owners, or project managers.

How you do this is email or call to set up a meet-and-greet for a proposal. Of course you should bring a few complimentary dishes of your best, but it's not obligatory. It will show good practice of faith. The key object is a professional presentation, using all eye contact, straight posture, dressed accordingly to pitch your proposal. The basis of your proposal should be to introduce your food truck to their venue for a trial run. You can leave references and your prior venue or event hosting and catering résumés.

Next you will show them why adding your food truck to their venue is a bonus and a plus that both parties can benefit from. For example, you would say that your food truck will cater and serve food and drinks to your employees at their location. Therefore, you won't have to worry about them being late from break clocking in or possibly a car accident, maybe even getting stuck in traffic with carpooling of workers. The venue and establishment will benefit with more convenience and being timely for your employee, plus it's all affordable dishes on the menu. Therefore, you show them why it's all beneficial for employees, attendees, and guests. Give them every plus of how you can help with your food truck being posted versus being a waste of space and time.

You also can use this point strategy with all venues. Just simply explain why the concertgoers will be more convenient by a food truck at their open-door venues because they don't have to travel outside venue, find and repark their cars, or worry about missing an event or performance. However, if you are more of an introvert, you can feel free to ask or get a type-A extrovert to pitch your proposal and presentation. Some will ask for a fee or percentage. It's up to you to negotiate.

Finally, you must remember to take into account the pricing on your menu board, decals, and lights outside your food truck. You need all of them to start-up, and they are essential for your food truck. You need big decals on the outside of your food truck or trailer. You can get those all less than $500. However, to get your whole truck wrap, it will cost usually around the $2,000 to $3,000 range. Developmental stages of your truck exterior should be built on your dish premise and food truck theme or brand always. Please remember, this helps you to enable your proof of concept and timely mistakes.

- Chapter 6 -

"Sanitation, Safety & Hazard"

In this chapter of sanitation, safety, and hazards, you really need to look at it as a food truck 101 course or operational safety prevention manual. We will go over some very important attributes and what not to do, or else your whole food truck business and reputation will be ruined, shut down, and quarantined. Maybe even potentially with a lawsuit, civil complaint, or a class action civil suit if you expose multiple people to bacteria or contamination.

This is what you must do in proper prevention after the Health Department Board does their initial inspection to maintain a healthy, clean, sanitary environment for your food truck, workstations and utensils, and employees along with all paying customers. It all goes hand-in-hand.

First let's begin with sanitary. Being sanitary is of or relating to health, period, or hygienic and being free from filth or infective matter. This is what you must first have, you and all your food truck employees practice before they learn to cook, work the fryer, or serve people, especially if they cooking and serving people by touching cash and dealing with the money. All hand-to-hand transactions need to be separate so you are not cross-contaminating germs or spreading bacteria by cross-breeding thru touching cash money while preparing and serving food dishes to the public.

Next you have sanitation. Sanitation is the number-one goal, and practice daily for the best sanitary results. Sanitation is the act or process of making sanitary. Also protection of health by maintenance of sanitary conditions. The key is to sanitize always before and after. Washing hands, using gloves, hairnets, beard nets, cleansers, and protective separate closed containers of foods and toppings. To sanitize is just to make sanitary or to make more acceptable by removing unpleasant features. You can even use sanitary wipe rags to keep your food stations clean or sanitary napkins, a disposable absorbent pad used to clean up spills and throw straight away. Even bacteria or raw meat juices or whatever you need to wipe down for cleanse. However, you must make sure all your employees don't leave sanitary wipe rags saturated in that same bucket or container from the day before, spreading or breeding bacteria.

Therefore, you need to be aware of all the ways to spread bacteria or germs in order to prevent and stop the spread or remove them. Contamination is to infect, soil, or stain by contact or association. This is what you have to be very careful and not to contaminate things or catch something that got contaminated and expose of it by termination. You must not reclean or reuse something once it's contaminated like a container or especially food. You must remember never to attempt to salvage food and extras from the day before. Just throw it away if you cannot give it away. Most food trucks use a restaurant kitchen or somebody's kitchen to pre-cook the majority of their dishes before parking at the location or their serving rush hours. This method of practice is all fair game, but you must not fall into a bad malpractice of attempting to store food in order to save money and inventory cost.

You will definitely get a lot of people sick, spreading bacteria of spoiled food. Instead focus on cooking just enough for that day you think your projection to serve people will be. Even if you are a little short or a little over, it's alright, and that over or under profit margin is better than a civil complaint suit or getting your whole food truck business operation shut down from contamination and getting people sick.

Keep all closed containers. Remember, don't expose raw food on food. It is also a such thing called airborne diseases, too. Pathogens can definitely spread by air like the flu. Pathogens are a specific agent as a bacterium causing disease. Food poisoning is highly possible, too, which is the worst review of your food truck start-up. If you have people online leaving bad reviews stating that your food truck made them suffer from food poisoning and sick as hell, all of your potential customers and market is influenced. Now you have a tainted food rep and possibly reported to the Health Department for violation and get your truck shut down permanently and lose your food handling license or food truck permit overall. Therefore, if you not aware of all the things, how can you fix or catch them? The only effective solution is to be proactive with great sanitation practices as a daily food truck ritual and employee regimen of hygienic, protection, and proper maintenance of sanitary conditions.

You must put up rules for workers and employees to keep food stations clean and spray and wipe down with proper sanitation, along with the rules posted up to follow by steps per entering the food truck to work, cook, and serve. Like the first step is to wash both hands thoroughly for 20 seconds. This is called the 20-second rule, which most physicians recommend to avoid spreading disease, bacteria, or pathogens. It cuts down by far and an effective measure of prevention. Next step is proper protection like hairnets, beard nets, gloves, and eyewear if necessary.

A warning sign that if you're sick, please don't come to work around food and contaminating the place. A small space pathogens can spread rapidly and breeds in warm environments like a cesspool.

The third step is employee integrity and accountability. This for them to be responsible for the good health and sanitary practice and work habits of uphold a service and obligation to all people, the customers and other co-workers. Also don't be afraid to run a training course in hygiene, sanitation, and safety after you hire employees or your extra helpers, even if it's friends or family that you having helping you out temporary with your physical initial start-up to get your food truck off the ground and going until business picks up to hire real employees. With this you can have any steps, tips, methods, and sanitary practices for your employees you see fit for your practical food truck. The main focus factor is for a great clean environment for all employees and customers. You just have to make sure all your employees truly value and is competent in sanitation practices. Throw all food away at the end of the day or give it away, but absolutely no recooking, rewarming, or reuse. Drill it into them no food salvaging or leaving food around and food crossing other raw foods.

Teach them about all the bacteria they can spread or create thru bad sanitation practices or negligence, including E. coli, which E. coli is a rod-shaped bacterium that sometimes causes intestinal illness and complications usually spread by contaminated food. Also salmonella, which is a similar of any of a genus of rod-shaped bacteria that causes various illnesses, especially food poisoning.

Now let's jump into the subject of safety. Truck safety is not just an emission test. It's for the safety all around the truck exterior and interior. All the staff and customers' safety and well-being. Not just safety from preventive sanitation ethical practices, but safe working environments, too, like your food truck having a hood and ventilation system to make sure it's not too smoky to see, serve, or for your health breathing. Even like having a commissary where you dump your oil and grease at. Parking is a major safety concern, too. You must be aware and very observant where you park your food truck. Make sure it's not putting people at risk or customers at risk to get hurt or hit by cars just to get a bite to eat. If you do park at a construction site for lunchtime, are you parked correctly and not in a construction hazardous zone of machinery and operations? You must assess the risk at all times as the owner, manager, and operator daily.

Safety is a sole responsibility to provide all freedom from danger, security, and provide a measure for preventing accidents or casualties. Again, without you as a food truck owner providing safety and safe, friendly environment, you are liable for civil lawsuits and formal complaints. These you can avoid at all costs even if you take the time to hire a safety consultant or expert to do a food truck walk-through before all inspections, openings, or operation drills. It's important to make sure and invest nobody gets hurt or injured too bad working for your truck. If you would suggest you good and got this safety part with a firm grip or game plan, I would suggest to you that you're wrong and misjudged, because it is a such thing as an accident-prone food truck with all type of safety violations and hazards, where that truck was deemed inoperable due to safety concerns and hazardous violations. Look at all the bad food truck reviews online. One I Googled and the whole food truck axle fell off. It's a whole listing pages you can scroll down to review all violations and learn what not to do, especially putting people and your business in jeopardy.

Hazards is last topic, but it is incorporated with safety. A hazard is a source of danger, risk, accident, or unsafe. Hazards are tricky because one day it's cool and running safe and accordingly. The next day it can pose an imminent hazard and danger. Therefore, you must train yourself to see and look for any risk, dangers, and hazards. Teach your staff the same way how to spot things unsafe that pose a danger and hazards to health and public. As a boss, manager, or business owner, it's your job to teach, lead, and bestow ethical practices. You cannot just simply hire a teenager because they are old enough to work a side gig without training and guiding them with or without prior experience and training, especially around tools, driving, cooking, like it's a hazard if your fryer employee don't know how to use a proper cutting knife on the board and chop a finger off accidentally. You're liable because you did not train them to use the utensils properly and safe. All need a training safety and hazard course. Also if they have an open cut of bleeding not to expose bloodborne disease or infection into the food dishes they're serving to the public. They must be taught accountability to secure, cleanse, and let someone know they are bleeding to take over. If that blood drops into the fryer or deep fryer, it's all contaminated food and utensils that need to be thrown out and resanitized. Look for all potential hazards.

Remember it's totally up to you and on you as the food truck owner to be very agile and vigilant when it comes time to safety and hazard prevention. You wouldn't park your food truck directly under an actual crane dangling at a construction site. Or you wouldn't let your employee dump hazardous chemicals or the red hazardous bag of bloody towels around the truck. Lastly, keep a first aid kit inside truck, and encourage your staff to take a CPR class for preventions. CPR certified is always the best safety bonus for your employees and customers. Also, fire extinguisher is mandatory for safety precautions and hazards, too. Finally, every food truck, Health Department requires a commissary to dump oil, water, etc., and to store a freshwater tank and separate tank for grey (used) water. Remember your responsibility is to identify all hazards and know how to prevent yourself from those hazards.

By getting a 3-part sink built by a plumber or manufactured, it's best to wash your utensils separate from the other operational sink stations. You can get this 3-part sink used, too.

- Chapter 7 -

"Building your Brand & Marketing"

Building your food truck brand is not complex. It is simply about bringing brand awareness. You create your niche dish, menu board, and complete mission is to build on that brand, make people aware of your food truck existence. Develop a great reputation for quality and customer service for the ultimate food truck experience. Then the whole objective is to build a customer base and genuine relationship for them to be repeat or regular customers. It's not just great food truck dishes, it's about the customer service and experience, period. If you can develop and build on that to perpetuate and innovate your customer service skills while providing that new experience to impact, cater, serve, and satisfy your customers all equally, you will continue to build upon your brand like a big household company or 5-star restaurant. Remember you don't have to have a 5-star restaurant to have 5-star reviews, and that is how you build upon that brand thru word of the mouth and referrals of great reputation for timely service and quality.

Let's start with building, first. What is your brand, goals, and mission? After you answer that what your brand is, means, and do well or renowned for, make sure to include the greatest: to help serve others and provide the ultimate experience. You must understand what building is, to enable to build a brand or have true brand awareness.

Building is classified under all these synonymous terms of equations. To increase, enlarge, enhance, to engage in building. To produce or create gradually. To bring into being or develop. Formed by ordering and united materials.

The key objective is to build your audience and connect. Focus on how to connect to them while breaking through to other audiences. One way to connect is thru your dishes because food is already a social connection and attached to a fulfillment and reward system from cravings. Therefore, you need to tap further into that audience exponentially and find different ways to engage by getting them involved in all your truck endeavors, new appetizers, locations, special tryouts all to reaction, response, and feedback, making them feel connected and part of the movement. A fan and consumer to build trust and loyal customer that will spread great reviews word of the mouth for you and organically. That is the aim in brand building, to build your community and allow them to grow and evolve with your food truck brand, too.

Once you tap into and discover your community, it's up to you to maintain quality and great customer service with a catering experience perpetually. You always look for more ways to build, increase, and innovate your brand. Do not stop because you feel your food truck has reached all possible success and brand is bigger than you ever could imagine. Popeyes did not stop once they hit a certain profit margin. Instead they created their chicken sandwich and introduced to their original audience and new audience and a global community frenzy of support and response. Therefore, you shouldn't stop because your brand is at the top spot for food trucks and known coast-to-coast. Instead continue to push, engage, and create new ways like Popeyes. Brand integration is even possible if it fits your brand, too. Don't forget you can tap into other ventures and markets pertaining to your food base or audience.

Influence in value and grow in popularity. Creators are the brands of the future because they find adaptable ways to connect their brands and connect with their audience or potential other new audiences. They generate traction by captivating people with their taste, style, and introduction to new dishes, new themes, new systems, and experiences.

There is really an art and science to brilliant branding. You must be adaptable to social promotions online and new generation tools, flexibility, and customization or specialization. Discerning is revealing insight and understanding, which is essential in brand building. Your brand is what the basis of your food truck and foundation stands on and grows on, usually based on your food truck dish and topic of what you serve. Maybe you have a brand slogan along with your brand messaging or mission statement. It can be a business motto or jingle. Catch vibes or theme songs goes viral quite often than you may think.

The real stories in business branding you selling a product or offering a service providing an experience is real causes, responses, and outcomes. All based on the engagement from the story you project with your why and their awe. The intention and energy you want, a huge idea that can become a big theme, message response, and massive branding unicorn all with the art of storytelling. It's about how you convey your story and message to convert traffic and customer to your food truck, message and backing your brand in full outpouring support. This is not a challenge, this part of brand building thru the art of storytelling is highly effective and a tool all big brands and ad agencies and informercials use to promote, push, or persuade people about their products, brand, or new services.

If you can't master the art of brand building thru storytelling, it's probably because your brand is too complex. I would suggest improvising and downgrading it or aim for simplicity. Make things simple. For example, you would not have a food truck sushi, egg rolls, hot dogs, cupcakes, and chicken-n-waffle theme. Mainly because it wouldn't fit into your brand, message, delivery, or slogan. It's way too much to promote and too much clutter. People like short, simple, easy, and instant gratification. They don't want to be confused with your brand identity, message, and what your main dish your brand specializes in. If they want sushi, they don't want to engage in a hot dog or chicken-n-waffle truck. You need to be transparent on your brand and the consumers need to be clear on what services you providing. They need to know exactly it is they're getting or their money going into, or else you will get dissatisfied customers and bad review rates, which again is totally opposite from brand building. It's called brand destroying. Just remember, simplicity is key. Think how can you simplify in branding or brand building as possible.

Simplification, empowerment, connection and community, transformation, quality, and top service all should be concoctions of your brand building process. Identity branding discovery, too. An element of testing what works or absolutely don't work by outsourcing and crowd-sourcing. You can test trials before introducing a new branding component you think that will work or fit within your brand. Reduce risk of implementations of new by testing product theories and concoctions to your menu and crowd-source before you build or spend on a product. Also co-sign on your signature brand as a new addition. See if users like, share online, or tell others about your new introduction product or dish to your food truck menu. You can provide and offer a different service than people are used to. Add a new element, bundling, once people see you have better prices and accessories. Maybe you can automate your services using technology and new tools to serve timely, faster, and more while affordable. You can even wrap your food truck and decals all in your brand or new menu item you branding. Remember you can use the data analytics and dashboards to help.

Next in branding and building is trigger theory, where you design great triggers of engagement loops to have people keep coming, engaged, and come back. Can you turn a customer into a family member of your food truck community and giving them a family-type orientation and experience thru your brand engagement and triggers? I believe you all can if you focus and understand your true trigger cues and points. For instance, it is visual cue trigger what people see, like great-looking delicious food and it will trigger your mouth to water or signal your brain craving system or stomach signal to rumble. Whereas, you have a sensory organ and sensory system that triggers you to engage in something thru stimulation, like sense by food triggers response by smell, or taste and visual. We eat with our minds as much as with our stomachs, too. The brain's amygdala and dopamine response, reward and memorable for food impression, especially if the food was great. The amygdala process food memory and how much you can consume and how satisfactory it was. Like take an appetizer, its purpose when you go to a restaurant before you order the main entrée. All an appetizer is a food or drink taken just before a meal to stimulate the appetite. Therefore, you want to make great triggers to stimulate and entice your audience to smell, order, crave, more and more feeding their reward system craving and taste of satisfaction. Therefore, once you choose a great tasting and smelling dish, you create a helluva brand presentation to further entice by cue triggers of senses that will appeal and appease to all consumers new and old to your brand.

Brand awareness and brand changes all should still coincide within each other and the realm of the brand basis. The same goes for cross-branding or brand integrating. It's just like Coca-Cola did with their logo, along with KFC, and Wendy's did, too. Over time they gradually made small changes versus one big brand change. That way they can evolve with the times versus having that same old original '60s and '70s version of their brand logo. Just Google the old Wendy's girl logo versus the new, along with the rest of your favorite brands. You'll see people don't like sudden changes. You have to do little adjustments, learn from branding mistakes of what works and what did not work. Then move on, focus, take some branding risks to test the waters, and reacting to the customer needs. Not being known for being a stagnant brand. Remember, design triggers with your signature brand that leads to good behaviors, outcomes, engagement, experience, and reward them, or simply convert them from a first-time customer to a lifetime customer to keep coming back for an exclusive taste and quality experience your food truck brand service provides. Maybe even to bring their family or a date is all possible with proper branding to convert all customer traffic lifetime members of your brand.

All you need to understand is brand is all about identity and connection. Branding is simply a class of goods identified as the product of a particular firm or producer. A distinctive kind. Match your brand to your specialization, entity, cause, and name, and you'll produce it systematically until it's automatically with brand innovating and upgrading in creativity. Remember to build energy and brand energy.

Marketing is to sell, produce, package, buy, trade, and the rate or price for commodity. A geographical area of demand for commodities. Marketing is also a strategy how you bring things and your message or brand to consumers, such as promotions, advertising, and including branding. Marketing and branding is similar and also go hand-in-hand. It's to advertise, inform, notify, and call public attention to especially in order to sell. Whereas, advertising is the business of preparing advertisements.

Top marketing is not hard or too complex, long as you know the main course of marketing strategies to formulate from. Also you can use your innovation and creative framework and tools just as you did with brand building optimization. The top marketing keys are number one, know your target audience, like gender, age groups, demographic, and geographical area. Number two, know what is important to them. Number three, know what they want, desire, and like or demand. Number four marketing tip is knowing how and why. You have to understand your audience, know them, and how to solve their problem effectively, quickly, easily. Then how to deliver that or convey that tool, message, service, or product item. You cannot have the fear of failing and what marketing nightmares that come with that, especially being a marketing blooper with your brand or affiliate branding.

We need to look for ways to market differently while keeping true to our brand and having brand integrity, too. Lastly, the name of the marketing game is making your target customers your exclusive marketers. That's it, nothing too complex or extravagant to understand. Again, with marketing, simplicity is the way to be. People need to be able to grasp your marketing concept and relatable to your brand identity as transparent as possible.

All in all your market target and cater to. Discover how to reach them and in different appealing ways. Then market further awareness and brand identity and tap into perpetually. You must really learn the effective system of delivering the appeal to local audience and outside your community, great taste, and affordable with great customer service. You must remember to cultivate your marketing with development. Even if the market conditions are up and down harshly. There should always be a market for what food service you offering. They don't buy what you do, they buy why you do. The why your dish is unique, tasteful, exclusive, and fulfilling. Convey your why first to inspire your food audience and targeted community. Then your marketing campaign will be complete and successfully.

- Chapter 8 -

"New vs. Used & Truck Maintenance"

Food truck variables. In this chapter we will show you the difference between new and used food trucks and food equipment. Then we will get into the importance of truck maintenance routinely and the cost.

Now that you got this far into the book and understanding how to actually start-up your own niche food truck business, we will show you how to pick out the right food truck for you, whether new, used, or customized to your cooking and kitchen needs.

It's important to have a business plan, too, because you can apply for microloans for minority and small business owners. They have government funding and start-up grants, tax incentive programs. You have to look online and research what all you qualify for to get your food truck revenue for operation, fees, license, and inspected permits. You can even do a crowdfunding and set-up a Kickstarter page to seek public help to kickstart your food truck start-up up off the ground by helping purchase the food truck you aiming for. You can also seek sponsorship and partners to help with all endeavors and assist with truck cost, or simply friends and family help and financial support. You still need a legitimate business plan for proper presentation and to look professional to be taken serious regardless if you cannot get an actual bank loan for your food truck. Also, like mentioned in the previous chapter, that your business plan should be written to act as a roadmap of operation to give you a close structure and real actualization of cost and all operations including overhead. Simply used as a great practice guide. It helps your outsource.

Now let's go over some pros and cons of new food trucks. It's mobile and reliable. What type of food? The core of basis of the menu and food equipment you want. It all depends to what type of a food truck you need, like a fryer, deep fryer, or burntop stove. Therefore, it needs to first fit and meet your menu needs that you have to serve and cater to. You don't want to fail health inspections because you boiling fish and all your menu items of raw food in same pot and utensils all day simply because the truck you purchase did not meet the cooking demands for your dish you chose to serve and build your menu off of. If you build your menu off your niche dish, then you should build your food truck off of your menu to serve. Basically you don't want to buy an old milk truck or sneaker mobile truck if it doesn't have a kitchen, cooking stations, and sinks in it.

Buying a brand new food truck, the risk is lower of repairs and breakdown. Also everything can be working but not properly or be working 6 months later. New trucks are built from scratch and customized with a guaranteed warranty. Plus it's appealing and looks new from the outside. You also can have your food truck wrapped and brand designed, including logos, contact info like numbers and all social handles, or simple decals, too.

The price of new food trucks can be fair expensive, from $70k upward to $250k. Again it all depends your kitchen needs and your customizations. I would say a full-size food truck with a nice fryer and burner stovetop with a 4 stainless steel sink with an 11k power diesel generator to power the whole truck, including a hood and nice ventilation system, plus rollout awnings, mist system and TV sound system will run about $160k new and custom-built to fit your kitchen style of choice. I recommend you look up new food custom truck online and check for all food truck manufacturers' reviews and history. I like a custom food truck manufacturer that does solid great work and has better reviews. It's located in San Antonio, Texas, named Crusine Kitchens. Go to crusinekitchens.com. Get your consultants or quotes, and look at all the work they do and the customization they specialize in, too.

Now the kitchen and layout will lend itself for what type of food. You must remember and consider this very important aspect or variable. Seeing the layout is very important to your food truck service and success. It's also a lot less decision making, stress, and situations. Decision making from what you already have versus need. Please don't attempt to make it just work with your kitchen truck layout if it doesn't fit. That's problematic and asking for trouble and complications of the truck, business, customers, and employees.

Now for a side note bonus for if you want to have an additional option. If a food truck is too complex or unaffordable, you can always start with a food stand. Then create enough revenue and scale to a food truck. Mobile food stands are inexpensive for start-up. You can post at different locations. Usually food stands are providing one service like hot dogs. They usually have one heater or cooker. You can go online and search these, too. Also some usually require a vendor's permit or registering a business license to sell the item. Again, check your local county and state requirements and do your thorough research like I've showed you how to in previous chapters also.

Let's step into the disadvantages of a used truck. I know you see all these pop-up ads stating how you can start-up a food truck business with only $5k for a used truck to fix up rock, rattle, and roll with cashflow. That's not realistic without no real problems. It sounds more like a Cinderella story. It can be a recipe for catastrophe.

You can spend $25k on used nice food truck and end up with $10k worth of damages repairs, maintain equipment, and mechanical wear and tear. Some companies don't want to build out or touch old trucks with new parts to add on simply because they don't want to be liable or tackle more complications when old parts go wrong with laboring, especially like the motor and suspension, etc.

You can also lease a food truck, rent it for lower payments, or another option is you can borrow a food truck to test the market. Google food trucks ready for business, they will resale products. Find a reputable food truck manufacturer site with feedback and reviews as a used food truck site, too. Additional features help, like sound systems, flatscreen TVs, retractable awnings, misting systems, and anything that brings attention to make your food truck appealing. Remember the more investments you put in and add-on features, the more you get back. The saying goes a long way: "It takes money to make money."

You can get yourself a truck used, buying it also on usedvending.com, too. Craigslist or eBay, also. Now, you must really be observant on buying used food trucks from cross country or neighboring states, because if it's listed for $3.5k but maybe don't start, you have to get it shipped, too. They could be just selling as is without a warranty or warnings. They don't include all the repairs needed or list all the problems with it mechanically or the kitchen and utility functions for operations or to pass inspections. Basically you have to be careful to not buy a used lemon or a shell of a food truck. You need to ask the right questions, do thorough investigations before purchasing or wiring money to ship. You can even Facetime with the seller and have them open up the hood, start it up, drive it, and see the kitchen layout and all features to see if they working properly. Of course if it's local, you can go to the seller and self-evaluate with your own checklist. Therefore, purchasing used out of state is a huge risk. It may be a super deal, but come with a super headache. Be leery of used deals too good to be true. That old saying is true, too, that you pay for what you get. Be careful of those fake food truck profiles and shipping scams, too, like sending you an invoice to purchase the truck and ship thru Amazon delivery service. However, it's all bogus and you'll never get the truck or it shipped. To avoid these used food truck purchase order scams, you need to make real contact, not just through via email. Get valid address, contact info, and locations you can confirm yourself. Usually if they don't want to speak or engage and FaceTtime, then it's probably bogus and a scam. This, again, is all the risk you run with getting used trucks.

Now, a bonus of buying used is that it's inexpensive so you can use it for buying used equipment, utensils, kitchen supplies. For example, fryers, air fryers, burner tops, sinks, ventilation systems and hoods, even awnings, shelves, countertops, and special features. You can get all these items online, too, at Craigslist, eBay, Facebook and local plumbers for sinks and installation your whole system, or electrician for running your wiring and power all locally. The ones doing side jobs outside of their profession are great hires and inexpensive. They help simplify things and specialize in them.

This is where you buy a used truck and it needs little affordable work to get it up and running to operate and pass inspections. If you can find you a decent pre-owned food truck for $7.5k and can find all the used equipment plus the installation cost under $3k, then you'll have met your under-$12k start-up budget. All this, again, is optional and based upon your menu board and the dishes you are cooking for your kitchen layout. Know that you understand this. You are officially ready to pick out your truck, build it up, and what works for you new or used.

Next I want to share with you the importance about truck maintenance. It's not just for emission and standard running. You want to make sure you do daily checks oil, gas, propane, and your powering sources. Your cooker and kitchen fully functional and maintenance all running properly. Make it routinely for servicing them at mechanic shops. Don't be cheap or neglect your truck just because the business aspect is thriving. If your truck is broke down or won't start, you can't get no money. It also may break down on a site you parked at and get towed and fined. Or you can possibly lose your vendor's and food operational license for zoning and timing violations.

Make proper decisions and take action to service your truck in confidence as being part of your food truck business success. Don't think because it's parked 90 percent of the time you don't need to work on service and maintenance regularly. Treat it like your kitchen and heart.

Finally, a full kitchen, full refrigerator, a 30-pound fryer and lid to keep oil in place. Also, the grill and griddle, oven, and 6-burner range are all options you can get built in to your truck new or used. Again, do what's suitable for your dish and caters to the menu that you're serving. The vent hood system that exhausts all the steam is required by code. The rinse and sanitize a hand-washing sink, too. With a shelf, you can have a microwave, also. A serving window and a service prep unit can also be new or used. Appliances can all run off of propane or electric and can run propane outside truck to the back of the truck.

It ranges anywhere from $40k for a basic trailer all the way up to $250k plus for a new built food truck customized, 9 ft. awnings that roll out, features like flatscreen entertainment and sound system draws crowds and holds customers in long lines. It's great for private crowds and events. People will call you to cater to their private crowd or events.

Remember you can build a trailer, buy equipment, the fryer, vent hood, etc. You can buy used or refurbished at 20 percent cost down versus new. Remember to research and search around different used websites or platforms and exercise your best options to coincide with your budget and realistic business plan. Also invest in the right generators for your truck new or used, too. Generators can power up the whole truck self-sufficient. Get your generators ran with the right electric power by professional local electrician. Your generators are essential to your electric power system or solar power source if you outsourcing.

You'll need two 200-pound propane tanks, especially if you have lucrative busy high-volume customer days or hosting events and venues. Next make sure your truck inside has stainless steel countertop and surfaces. Also you can get a 2-fryer that can fry up to 4; 2 fryers should be enough because each fryer has 2, which equals a total of 4 fryers for the truck cooking stations. Then, make sure it's in compliance when you get inspected by Health Department.

- Chapter 9 -

"Hosting, Event Planning, & Social Media Promo"

A host is one who receives or entertains guests, or a server. Therefore, hosting is what you are doing when you are serving people from your food truck, or better known as catering your services to people. The aim in this category is to be the best at hosting and the top at your food truck hosting class to get picked or referenced. You can also be known for hosting big events annually, seasonal, or on demand where your food truck caters to an enlarged crowd or target audience. We went over some of these tactics and angles in previous breakdowns in the chapters' chronological orders.

You want to be on your A+ game of service, speed, and quality taste. Most of all, time management and management skills. Being able to properly manage or hiring proper food truck management is very important to be able to manage hosting and events at venues. The functioning aspects of moving on demand at high speeds for sustainable durations. Some events can go from 12 p.m. to 12 a.m., a 12-hour hosting event. Can your food truck, employees, and inventory keep up with all needs for the complete time? You must take this into consideration before you start to tackle hosting huge events for long-time duration. It can be very intense. Also just because you or your management did a successful smaller hosting event doesn't mean you and management can endure bigger venues' intensity.

Lobbying is a group of persons engaged in lobby and to try to influence public. Therefore, lobbying doing scheduled lunch, breakfast times with companies or huge entities, warehouses, and any events or establishments. During your lobbying, you can introduce your food truck and new specific dishes. You can feature new appetizers or do specials like a buy entrée and get one of your choice free. This will allow them to taste different dishes and a better chance for a great-tasting dish to hook them or convert them into a lifetime customer. Some people can just be simply fans of your food truck or theme. For example, they may be a vegan or on keto but love the idea theme of your truck and your unique concoction of dishes like a chicken-and-waffle cupcake or just a cool old school recipe from the family cookbook you brought into the presence. During lobbying, you'll meet brand-new people in the public, so it's your job to leave a great first impression of food taste, time, and quality service. The aim is to connect with as many people during lobbying as possible and leave them with a taste of great experience.

Next it is event planning. Before you plan any event to host, you must properly probe for the event. Getting with all your workers to see if they are available beforehand. Also if you utilizing other people's business kitchen to pre-cook to kickstart your day to get ahead of the demand, they need to be contacted prior, too. Sharing kitchens is a valid solution. However, if you land a hosting gig at a huge event or venue, you can run into problems of schedule conflicts if you need their kitchens for longer durations prepping. Make sure you have enough supplies like cups, styros, plastic forks and spoon, napkins, etc. Check your propane tanks and power sources like generators. Make sure your truck is totally operational from the kitchen to driving. Basically inside out.

Event planning you should offer walk-throughs of your truck or offer virtual tours online to show them your truck inside out and your services you cater. It's a great bonus tip if you add on your tour site how many of people you can service and cater to by hour or just your analytics on service rates. Be diversified with all your parts you list on your itinerary system. An itinerary is the route or routine of a journey or the proposed outline of one, or simply a guidebook. You mainly want to convey your max service and capacity. You want to guarantee your quality and customer service. Some of the best event planners and promoters have mastered the art of show and tell. They offer you all what they can do along with their why they can do it. Then they show you by providing services they guarantee.

Usually, you can offer incentives like giving discounted rates or bonuses to event promoters and managers for booking your food truck for cater and service to the crowd and audience for the whole duration of the event activities. However, on the other side of that coin, you can demand your certain stipulations and bonuses from your great reputation of service, skills, time management, and quality. Then you wouldn't have to offer discounts.

You can get on people's and companies' email list, follow them, and put your service you offer for hosting events on all online service and entertainment platforms. Also again, don't be afraid to go out on a limb doing cold calls, converting cold traffic and doing random emails about your brand awareness and services you host. Most people don't know how to network to find work and placement, but you have to believe and have energy to make it thru those thresholds to break through to entities and events with marketplaces and venues. Whatever you focus on, you will feel and penetrate to achieve them. You already have a gateway into social engagement with providing a food service. There are many deals made, love initiated, and alliances or friendships over a dinner and eating a hot meal. Great food is fulfilling, satisfactory, and a joyful and sense of calm to help you reset and refill up with energy. Food is essential just like water to live. Therefore, food always provides value no matter what. So you cannot be timid or embarrassed to make contact and break through. Your dish is the opening topic of discussion and then your services, features, and customer service.

Remember food is a power source, just use all your resource within you to provide expression of food, love, and services to network hosting angles for proper event planning. Prioritize diversity and how you specialize in working with intensity like a raving concert crowd that's maybe super pumped up or buzzing tipsy drinking alcohol. Show that the customer always right and smile when they being belligerent and yelling or blaming you for getting their order wrong. This is how you impact and influence event organizers of your quality customer service and dealing with all diverse crowds for catering with professional skillsets. Have a process in place to deal with certain behavior and customer engagement. Once you get your food truck known for greatness and form businessships and venueships, they will demand you to cater and phone will be ringing perpetually. People will call you for events, concerts, business locations, catering, churches, outside live events, and so on.

Let's get into social media promotions. Your online presence is everything nowadays, especially if you want to be successful for your turnouts. You should be registered on all social platforms. Twitter, LinkedIn, Facebook, SnapChat, Instagram, Pinterest, and you can even have your food truck's own YouTube channel. Social media presence helps drive your audience to you and the events you hosting or where you parked at for the weekend. It's also to influence them or entice them with your food dishes, like a Wendy's commercial advertised food. It's brand awareness, too, by identifying who you are and what you specialize in. Most all fan and consumer engagement to stay relevant and in their feed daily. You never know when your dishes' photos or daily story posted and SnapChats trigger someone into a craving that's already hunger. Once you drive that desire with that food trigger, they will run to your food truck to reward their hungry cravings for great savory or sweet taste. Remember, be adaptable to new generational tools and social media, e-devices, and platforms they are on to use for a way to connect, tap in, and push your food truck dishes.

It helps target your audience, demographic, and locations easier, especially if you use the data analytics and learn how to crunch the data and read the algorithms to find all your niche audience, and a specific crowd who loves eating your type dishes. You no longer have to do long intensive annoying surveys or bothering people for their spare time to answer a long list of questions. Those days are long over with thanks to data, which is the new oil, especially for businesses and small business owners to help deliver a better service and know exactly what they want, love, or like to consume. Data basically gives you a spreadsheet/cheatsheet with all the survey and metrics or statistics you need to function your business correctively and accordingly. Like saving you time and money on cooking service or inventory that your audience simply don't want or like. If you serving more fish tacos than carne tostados, you wouldn't make the mistake by preparing the equal amount of carne tostados that won't make an equal return on your investment of time and money. Therefore, using the data is your best policy. You can use Facebook, for example, with their ads for effective targeted audience results at an cheaper rate to run your ads or promote your content to.

The whole reason is to get social awareness, letting people engage back with your food truck brand, leaving comments, reviews, and compliments. You can follow them back, answer questions, and engage back with your community. Then, watch how much it grows, and your following and likes increase, or your videos shared, retweeted, or tagged. You will neglect your personal social media pages because you will be so busy with your food truck brand of social platform engaging. Again it's letting people know when exactly you going to pull up or be at their city and locations. They all should include timeframes, dates, name of events or venues, and exact cross streets locations.

Using the digital apps like Twitter, you can alert people where you parked at for the day. Facebook certain events you can convert traffic. Instagram is great for brand awareness short videos and showcasing pics of your food, services, and events. This is all building content. It's a little of creating content, but not creative content because you already have the content created within your dish, truck, theme, and brand. It's totally about how you formulate it geniusly for marketing, advertising, and conveying your unique message or selling point digitally and socially on a huge platform for a larger world audience. Even Facebook food truck groups.

Even if you are not too social media engaged or tech savvy and like using apps, you can hire someone well enough experienced to engage with the audience and run all your social feeds, time, dates, events, and locations, including any new add-ons or special services and celebrity-packed events to integrate both your audience and their fans or crowd. This is the social aspect.

- Chapter 10 -

"Franchise & Multiple Food Trucks"

In any corporate business, especially with an IPO, their whole aim is to be acquired by a larger company and split the profits of selling their business with shareholders of the company or any investor from angels to private loan sharks or equity and license of purchase orders.

However, for microbusinesses and small business owners or minority business first-time owner, the whole aim and end game goal is to franchise their company. To be able to have more than one business in different areas, cities, or countries. To multiply all your main base premise of operations from your already proven success system and data with cashflow lucratively. Then it's joint ventureship of being a franchise and offering your business for other first-time owners or all people to rep and operate your brand with you. Everyone should want to take their food truck and business to the next level and soar to the highest of eagle heights. Exponential growth is what your whole business objective is behind your why. Growth is mandatory and any business can grow if you learn how to manage it successfully and all your power points versus pain points while learning to spot all your potential growth areas and sources. Some people fail miserably at this and business because they are simply not putting in the real work, triple-time, and applying the right aspect and leadership skill it takes to troubleshoot and problem solve. Most people and business owners make the dire mistake and don't expect the unexpected in business, including with unexpected expenses that cripple their business with consumed debt.

A franchise is a right or license granted to an individual or group, or a constitutional or statutory right or privilege. A franchisee is one who you granted a franchise. The franchiser is one who grants or gives a franchise.

A Wing Stop or KFC food chain is all franchises. Along with multiple entities including sports, dealerships, all large household brand-name businesses. They all work in functional multi-unit operations franchise gurus.

For example, after your food truck grows, you will be able to be a franchise and give exclusive rights for a fee upfront and a royalty for using your brand name and product that you have successfully developed into a renowned brand to an individual or individuals called a franchisee. You want people to operate independently as a franchisee. Maybe one day you can be CEO that takes your food truck franchise public for IPO and people to buy shares of stock in your food truck company. Remember that's the whole big aim to franchise.

However, you can also be a turnaround entrepreneur. Not by flipping food trucks. One that turns around already failing food truck businesses. Just like Bar Rescue does, it works for a profit and a great reputation to build on. Therefore, a food truck rescue can possibly be more your speed versus attempting to franchise or have the responsibility and full-time duty of running multiple food trucks and managing them and your brand representation all at once. It can be over-assertion. Some people are born to handle multiple things at once, others are meant to handle one thing in front of them at a time. Do not attempt to overload your caseload or take on more than you can do. Maybe you're more knowledgeable about how to run a successful food truck and can help manage that and help people turn around their already existing truck. You can troubleshoot immaculate and have a gift to problem solve and consult with other truck owners.

If you have conflict in the room, then come up with a resolution and hold each other accountable. That is the mindset and skillset to lead and manage successfully. Then how to simplify the process and minimize it to reduce to make things easier. The risk and return.

Then you have time management. It's prioritizing what's important and doing it daily. Having people help you to do the small tasks. Hiring help, little things that's time consuming, online, emails, and driving to places commuting. Also setting up your day and scheduling to-do list. Prioritizing it is key to franchising and running a successful operation and team. A lot of people overthink and overprocess versus simplifying, prioritizing, and time management.

Now I want to give you an overall prospective outlook of franchising of a blueprint, for example, so you can see the transformation and mentality it takes to start within planning, developing, and seeking your goal.

Music mogul Dr. Dre Billion Dollar Blueprint he created people to cultivate his gift putting them in front of his audience like Tupac, Snoop, Eminem, and 50 Cent. Then placed headphones around his audience for his billion-dollar exit. Even his artists and other artists wear his Beats by Dre headphones for that trusting great quality sound and brand for ultimate Dr. Dre experience with music of their choice.

This is a way for to look at how you want to start out with your end goal or exit plan to franchise concept, too.

Now that you understand what franchising is and how to, I'll show you how to start off and scale your truck into multiples. No one would not believe in your business or invest in your franchise if you cannot provide real data and proof of concept as your food truck brand is profitable. You cannot just do these metrics from one merely truck. It is best to have multiple food trucks in multiple areas. Your turnaround rate, process rate, serve time rate, and product rate all have to be proven. Same for your customer ratio of craving taste and customer service base. That great dish and your great customer service skills and management operation all need to be proven and shown over a valid period of time. Years, month record of profits and proceeds need to be available for comps to potential franchisee investors to your truck franchise. This is all the essential steps you need to have established in order to have a valid system to solidify your franchise success valuation.

Let's get further into ways to build your truck brand to get multiples. Again, get your truck out there and have your brand awareness building momentum and posting new content daily online. Build your brand further, hand out wristbands, cups, etc., and keep people all over town with your food truck brand in their mouths. You need patience and passion.

Next, get parking anywhere safe, or buy a lot to rent out for supplying parking to other trucks. Also, additional space for all your trucks new and old. Remember, it's all about generating positive consistent cashflow and clientele. Therefore, by creating bonus, extra, or side cashflow besides your day-to-day food truck operation is what helps you to scale and enables you to buy another food truck to imply your same food service and successful method of operations. It's actually fun franchising and build up the momentum and revenue to do so. It's also one huge self-challenge that's great to test to see, can you maintain your business with nice margins thru all the trials, errors, and obstacles that arise. It will keep you busy at a steady pace to balance including all your work and staff ethics. Parking is a plus because when you not serving, you need to have your truck or trucks parked somewhere and safe. The same for other food truck owners, too.

Next method to scale is guerrilla marketing, known as ground-and-pound marketing. Hit the ground running a marathon race at a sprinter pace. Go where everybody goes to lunch, warehouses, lunch hours period and hand out food truck flyers. Flyers are great branding awareness and a great marketing tool. You can reach more people in parked areas, or vast locations such as plazas, malls, or place of employment. Usually they are already hungry or thinking of a place to go eat. Therefore, flyers can entice and break through effectively to people.

Another element to scale you can expand your food truck business outsourcing using a delivery service, like DoorDash or other apps delivery services provided that fit and will pick orders from your truck. This offers better sustainability and reaching more people to make more revenue to increase cashflow rapid and during more hours. Or another option is you can actually start your own delivery service for your own trucks and deliver other trucks' food, too. That way you will get your delivery cost from your customers, along with charging other food trucks a delivery service fee, too. This can all be done as extra add-on features to your truck nobody else has or uses in your areas and zones as an effective option. You have to think outside the box to scale outside the box and franchise. Even if you try a delivery service with your food truck for a short period duration as a test run, I guarantee you will see satisfaction results and a margin increase of your truck flow.

The most successful people have the strongest principles and ethics of business operations. Some people are against this next one or too ashamed of the crowd it generates because they want to serve a more wealthy crowd or fanbase. However, it is doing a pay options with all your customers to be able to pay with EBT. It should not be no discrimination with how your customers pay for food with cash, debit, or EBT. Most people don't want to accept food stamps with their food truck or have EBT association. All customers should be welcome including their paying method. I would do EBT acceptance and advertise it as well along with a sign up by the menu board, too. If you choose to accept EBT, your cashflow and customers will definitely increase, too. EBT converts to dollar-to-dollar, not only 50% or half off the dollar amount. It will convert into the cash amount total of the purchase order, and the government gives you the full cash amount. Therefore, while other food trucks are biased about accepting EBT or their crowd of customers it brings. However, if you accept EBT, you will scale faster to help assist your other financial endeavors to get multiple trucks up and running that, too, can all accept EBT to franchise. Just leap.

Lastly, you can do a kitchen at home cooking service for a food delivery service that you don't have to have a whole restaurant space or even a food truck. You can cater to family and friends on Facebook or social media that want your dishes and willing to pay for your specialties. People do enjoy take-out delivery, it's more convenient, beats traffic, parking, and their time.

You can even find a food truck mentor to get practical advice to focus and get started on your franchising to make it into an effective action and a sure reality. From finding matching teams and management that fits with your patterns, methods, and brand principles, that drives your truck growth success, including how to decode customer service and structures. How to use data to increase successful systems, and customer acquisition. You need to be team centric, empower and support with accountability to all your franchisees and show them how to work and run the operation to achieve success start-up versus failure. They need to be clear and a real problem solver. Remember sweat equity and resources go long ways. You want someone to have a shared vision and passionate to franchise to.

- Chapter 11 -

"Customer Service"

This final chapter of this food truck start-up blueprint, I wanted to leave you with the importance of customer service and break down some elements of positive customer service. You want to be known for your food truck being customer-friendly and cater towards all customer needs, too. I cannot put enough emphasis on customer service. Customer-centric is the whole success to your operation beside your actual dish you serving. If your customers are not satisfied, they will not come back and will leave bad reviews on your services. You need to make customers feel welcomed to come back by providing them with an experience of great customer-friendly service. You need to be a social butterfly and people person to engage and give people customer experience. Train all your staff to be people person with great customer service skillset you bestow in them with your food truck ethic and code of customer conduct and principles. For example, a code of customer conduct will be to tell your employees, if someone gets mad at you, time, or order mix-up and mess-up, you kill them with kindness and always smile and say okay. Tell the customer they are always right.

Challenging maintain customer base. Working with customers and public needs. "Customer is right" should be every food truck's open-door policy of operations. People will get aggravated waiting for food or having a long and bad day. However, after a great manner customer service friendly and customer courtesy and after they ate food, it's all worth the wait. Most people will calm down after they ate and settled down. Just like the Snickers commercial where they act out and turn into somebody else until they feed their Snickers crave. Also additional add-ons like misters, mobile benches, and standing bars with umbrellas for outside shade. The food truck should always provide a safe, comfortable customer environment. Plus for the people to eat, relax, and option to order some more besides drink refills. Remember, offer your workers a high-impact customer service and engagement training experience. If the employee is more introvert, maybe they should just cook rather attempting to do customer development skills. Everything or position is not for everybody. It's your job to manage right as a leader and food truck coach. You have to see what engagement works and what don't. Same for the employees and pieces of puzzle for your food truck success, what works and fits versus what don't fit and won't fit your service needs or brand. It's about the customers' demand and voice of what they want, need, and asking for constantly. Maybe even adjustments towards their needs, demands and wants. You cannot ignore your customers' voices because they help your brand grow and get better. That's your improvise to success approach and evolvement as a brand.

Quality and customer service should be your food truck number-one goal and aligned with your mission statement. You can do a stress test to see how your staff/team and food truck do with new menu and pressure while bestowing in your new customer service ethics and principles for quality, speed, coverage, and servers. This temporary test will show your staff weak points and what part of customer acquisitions they need to improve in a customer manner friendly. Remember toxic people and environments is crucial, including a toxic work environment. Toxic-free is the way to be for interior and exterior of the food truck environment.

Next is customer intimacy. Knowing your customers, what they want, like and how to deliver it. How can you differ with your approach? It's about the guest satisfaction. You must be managing properly. You can have customer service questioners on paper or request them give you a Google review on your customer service skills, quality, and timing all in one. You can place a sign or decal request all customers the right to engage in customer service reviews or complaints to your email, via mobile business line, or on your social platforms. You never ignore what your customers are asking, saying, or complaints about. The ideal in customer intimacy is to let them know and to show them they all matter and their services matter, too, as top priority. Feedback is what you want and you should use to pivot your business forward. Positive feedback or constructive criticism feedback, too. All feedback is welcome. I cannot express how important the essence of real feedback in real time is for your food truck business or multiple trucks.

Customer intimacy is a very close association or an intimate friendship association. I wanted to be clear not to confuse or intimidate thinking of customer intimacy as couples or partner intimacy, especially for all the younger readers to mistake the word intimacy for being the same type as boyfriend and girlfriend intimacy. Instead it's just a closeness to your audience, crowd, food truck fans, and lifetime customer you gained to keep coming back to your truck and order more. Then focus in and concentrate on all that intimacy thru engaging and interactions. Simplify by summing up all what you have learnt and gained thru all of it for ultimate results by connecting more with customers at their preference and speed. You must tap in your audience and market with customer intimacy engagement to make those connections. If you cannot make customer connections, how will your food truck stay in valid business or have any standard reviews like the other trucks in your area or city and state does? Remember it is not a race. However, it is a competition on a huge food, catering, and delivery service marketplace, especially with household brands and huge entity distributors. Therefore, always ask yourself, How can you always be more customer intimate? How can I find better ways, evolve, and grow with customer association and closeness daily?

Customer experience. Ultimate customer experience is the aim and number-one goal daily when they visit your food truck. It could be a first-time guest or a regular customer. Customer experience is to finding the experience your customer needs, wants, talks about. How can you make a different experience that works and create new ways? How can you continuously build on customer experience? This is all what our focal points and pain areas should be construed on always.

You want to make your audience accustomed to great customer service experience with your food truck brand. Accustom is to make familiar through use or experience. Customer acquisition is just something that is acquired by the customer or demand by. Therefore, acquired is, again, gained by or as a result of effort or experience. Your business model should absolutely possess all these qualities, no questions asked. If not, you should do a personal checklist and a to-do list. Then a mental adjustment note to elevate your business for customer experience greatness while providing the ultimate food truck experience. What does your food truck specialize in? That should also be included or provided by your customer experience category, too. You can check around with other people or check the online reviews of other food trucks similar to yours or same geographics and see what are all the customers saying through personal experience with those trucks. Then you evaluate, look at your food truck and what your fans and audience say about your customer experience you provide. See what all they mention. For instance, do they comment on your timing, services, taste, theme, or brand thru their experience?

There is also a such thing called over-commitment to creating the wrong or invalid customer experience. If your whole aim is to create a bond and impact thru your customer experience that you innovated or integrated that simply does not fit as you thought and would like it to have, then you need to make a few adjustments or possibly throw out that policy and start up a new providing experience, especially if your customers don't like the add-on or fit. Use the metrics to see what works with them. If your employees are reporting to you that the customer response and reaction is not so great or killing your return rate, then you should listen to your workers and kill your new product or service feature that the crowd and fanbase is rejecting. Even though you wanted them to accept it, you must get rid of it if they do reject it. You can win all customer service experience values you bestow or attempt to offer to the public for positive results. For example, if a person is used to having it a certain way, certain theme, or imagery, it will be harder for you to introduce or implement something new or odd, like ordering a Coke with their burger and fries. It's habitual and their norm with that brand like Burger King. Now go to Burger King attempting to buy a drink only without burger or fries. It would seem odd or out of place and possibly make you hungry and want to order a number 2 and 4 from their value menu. On the other hand, you wouldn't offer egg rolls with each value meal to give them a better or different customer experience if it does not fit and the customer frowns at the option or simply turns down your additional new egg roll offers. Remember customer acquisition and value.

Pay attention to all your audience, including your online traffic, too. Value, visions, mission, and solutions should all be consumer-based. The true value of offering experience thru socialization and bonding is priceless. The bonding over food should give customers experience they like and need for engagement, interactions, and fulfillment like a restaurant does by allowing into a nice clean customer service and food-friendly environment. Creating that great bonding experience needed with co-workers, family, or significant others. Remember food is just like music with your moods. It alters their consciousness. Therefore, it makes it more durable to bond, relax, listen, and engage with others a lot more in tune and clear.

This is exactly the customer experience you want to create for your targeted audience. You want to use that same big-brand restaurant mentality to provide great customer experience to your food truck business. You can wrap it all in your theme to give the ultimate food truck experience with that same restaurant point of view and successful guideline. It's all about your customers to have a successful food truck start-up. Good luck, and use this book as a study guide.

Finally, some bonus tips and overview to leave you with in the closing of this book's final chapter.

When people always start calling you and doing contracts busy catering multiple events, busy catering schedule, you need to be able to love people, talk to people, and a flat-out people person. Plus know how to cook and be good at cooking. Remember to test your food first for honest feedback to see if they will eat your food and come back to your truck again. Also it's thousands of Taco Tuesdays, pizza, wings, fish and chips food trucks all over. You need to really offer something truly unique or a new niche dish with a genuine recipe.

Deal great with pressure. Do a stress test with your truck and workers with a hundred-yard line. Remain calm, get food out, and move on. It's not a good business for you to start-up a truck if you don't like stress. It's not a good environment for you, especially if you don't have great people skills and like to deal with customers. Customer base, long hard hours and intensity is the challenge you facing daily. You must be aware of these challenges and obstacles and optimistic about tackling them before you put all your time, money, and resources into a food truck start-up. Once you have it all laid out, take effective action of your business plan to execute and scale accordingly. You must become a hospitality expert and value great customer service ethics.

Now you have successfully read this complete book and ready to tackle and begin your proper start-up efficiently. Don't be afraid to reread or listen to this book Audible the chapter and things you need to know, help, or apply with your food truck start-up!

About Author

Hitachi Choparazzi is a New York City native, by the way of Omaha, who is currently incarcerated in level 5 solitary confinement in Florence, SMU-Eyman Complex, serving an illegal sentence awaiting on Supreme Court Appeal to correct his sentence with time served. The error forces him to serve 2 years extra.

He is an entrepreneur, tattoo artist turned author. Also the sole owner of Chop-a-Style Publishing and Productions, and the owner of Chatmon Sr. Literary Agency. He has written over 20 books and including scripts to pitch to Netflix. All this while he was incarcerated to start his reform act.

Founder and CEO of Billion-Dollar Blueprint and the BDB movement/youth movement, an innovator entrepreneurship where he believes everyone has their own blueprint, like everyone has their own unique thumbprint. Based on 3 core principles—Education, Elevation, and

Innovation—which he teaches the youth and people how to format and discovery key. BillionDollarBlueprintmerch.com

The face of lockdown society movement along with the voice of lockdown society movement. IncarceratedLivesMovement.com #ILM #BDB

"I do this for y'all. I love y'all, rep y'all, and believe in y'all! I won't stop giving y'all all the raw stories as God bless them in my head. I have a hundred of them up there. Anybody that has a hot hand, send me samples or any comments, suggestions to my FB, IG Hitachi Choparazzi or email: orders@chopastylepublishingllc.com Chop-A-Style Publishing LLC and Productions. TeflonLuv!"

Hitachi Choparazzi prides himself on having his own signature Chop-a-Style where he freestyles all his books. They all rhyme with innovation and original storylines. He writes prequels, sequels, trilogies, and more. Does it for the people who love to read and for all those incarcerated in state, federal B.O.P., county, and women's facilities. FB,IG,Tiktok, Twitter, YouTube-Hitachi Choparazzi

Emails: Hitachichoparazziauthor@gmail.com
Billiondollarblueprintmerch.com

Chop-A-Style Publishing and Productions LLC

Other Books and Scripts by the Author

Non-Fiction

- How to Rap; The Elementary Teaching of Hip-Hop

- How To Tattoo & Start-Up Business

- How To Digital Detox

- How To Start-Up a Food Truck Business

- How To Stop School and Mass Shootings: Dear Parents

- Incarcerated Lives Matter: The Hitachi Choparazzi Blueprint

- How to Love

- The Switch: A Social Awareness Self-Help

- Nipsey Hussle Lockdown Society Dedication–Tribute

- If Trayvon Martin Could Talk; Injustice

Fiction

- The Eagle and Weasel (1-5 series kids' book)

- She Go! (urban novel)

- Reality Show 3D-HD (urban novel)

- Hot Thots (urban novel)

- Liqz (urban novel)

- Paranormal Whisper (horror novel)

- Pimp of Da Ratchets (urban novel)

- Pimp of Da Ratchets II Vegas (urban novel)

- Pimp of Da Ratchets 3 Orange is Da New Pimp (urban novel)

- Hitachi (urban novel)

- Penitentiary Pimp (urban novel)

- Weasel Society (urban novel)

- The Big Pep and Plucker Story-She Go! Prequel (urban novel)

Screenplays/Scripts

- Top Notch

- Hot Thots

- Pimp of Da Ratchets

- Weasel Society

- Million Dollar Games—A Secret Society

- The Eagle and Weasel (animation)

Available at Barnes and Noble and Amazon

Welcome to the exclusive lives of 4 extremely hot THOTs. This book will show you how to spot a THOT. From THOT tops to THOT flops, all the way to THOT Snaps and claps.

This book is the first-ever with a double twisted love triangle. Watch as Chicago, LA, ATL, and Seattle THOTs entwine at Coachella.

Some on fleek and some looking cheap, but they all cheat! They all commit aTHOTery with their THOTery acts, shameless.

Raunchy, with steaming hot sex scenes to sex swings. From wild threesome ménages, and twerking, to bare-it-all raw. Too hot! THOT gum pop...

This page-turner is an eye-opener to the very end, with a bombshell-dropping, shocking ending. The secret life of THOTs

Available at Barnes and Noble and Amazon

Billion Dollar Blueprint is a movement we challenge and inspire you to find your individual blueprint. Our mantra is "We believe everyone has their own blueprint like everyone has their own thumbprint". With these three core principles

Education

Elevation

Innovation

Hitachi Choparazzi is the founder and CEO. Orders available to support incarcerated businesses.

Orders available at: billiondollarblueprintmerch.com

www.ingramcontent.com/pod-product-compliance
Lightning Source LLC
Chambersburg PA
CBHW060346130626
46553CB00003B/1104